MIRACLE BREAKTHROUGHS
Volume I

Topical Devotions
for Him or Her

by:
Sara Zimmer

Published by:
Explosive Breakthrough Publishing, LLC
www.ExplosiveBreakthrough.org

MIRACLE BREAKTHROUGHS
Volume I

Copyright © 2016 by Sara Zimmer

Foreword copyright © 2016 by Chuck Zimmer

All rights reserved.

This book, or parts thereof, may not be reproduced in any form, stored in a retrieval system, or transmitted in any form by any means (electronic, mechanical, photocopy, recording, or otherwise) without prior written permission of the publisher, except as provided by United States of America copyright law.

Scripture quotations marked "NAS" are from the New American Standard Bible, copyright © 1960, 1962, 1963, 1968, 1971, 1973, 1975, 1977, 1995 by The Lockman Foundation. Used by permission. (www.Lockman.org)

Scripture quotations marked "KJV" are from the King James Version of the Bible (public domain).

Scripture quotations marked "MSG" are from *The Message: The Bible in Contemporary English*, copyright © 1993, 1994, 1995, 1996, 2000, 2001, 2002. Used by permission of NavPress Publishing Group.

Scripture quotations marked "NLT" are from New Living Translation, copyright © 1996, 2004, 2007, 2013 by Tyndale House Foundation. Used by permission of Tyndale House Publishers Inc.

Scripture quotations marked "CJB" are from The Complete Jewish Bible, copyright © 1998 by David H. Stern, published by Jewish New Testament Publications, Inc. (All rights reserved. Used by permission.)

ISBN-13: 978-1530219032
ISBN-10: 1530219035

Book Layout and Cover design by:
Kenny Mock, Mended Heart Music, Sapulpa, OK
www.MendedHeartMusic.com

Published and distributed by:
Explosive Breakthrough Publishing, LLC
PO Box 2522
Broken Arrow, OK 74013
www.ExplosiveBreakthrough.org
info@explosivebreakthrough.org

"As the cover of this book illustrates the many facets of God, I have seen the reflection of God's love shine through Sara over the past 16 years I've known her. This book is topically based upon the times and seasons of God for your life, and will bless you on a daily basis."

Rev. Larry G. Bishop
Senior Pastor
Dove Ministry, Inc., Jenks, Oklahoma

* *

"Sara Zimmer worships God with all of her heart, soul, and might. Her devotionals are inspirational and encouraging. Sara's insights arise out of a depth of love and intimacy with God as Abba Father. You will be both uplifted and challenged."

Dr. Paul King
Pastor, Author, and Professor

MIRACLE BREAKTHROUGHS

DEDICATION

This book is first and foremost dedicated to my Heavenly Father, for He is my life. Walking hand in hand with You, Daddy God, is a daily treasure. Your daughter adores You!

Next, I want to honor my parents, Chuck & Ruth Zimmer. Your support, encouragement, and example to put God first and seek after truth has been a foundation for my daily life. You have given me the greatest gift...a hunger to commune with Heavenly Father. Thank you! I love you both!!!

Lastly, this book is dedicated to you, the reader. While you read each day, may you experience joy on your journey as your fellowship grows and deepens with Abba God.

Table Of Contents

Acknowledgments iii

Foreword v

A Note From The Author vii

Chapter One - Love 1

Chapter Two - Peace 39

Chapter Three - Joyous Praise 75

Chapter Four - My Beloved 111

About The Author 149

Appendix A: Scripture References 151

ACKNOWLEDGMENTS

I have had many friends along the way who have encouraged me to publish my writings. You know who you are. I pray Heavenly blessings upon you for your gifts of friendship and faithfulness. You too will reap the rewards for the lives that are touched as a result of your support!

I want to acknowledge and thank my pastors, Larry & Linda Bishop, along with my church family at Dove Ministry. You have showered me with love and prayers and encouraged God's destiny for my life. May you reap abundantly for all you have sown!

Many thanks to the Mock family for your friendship:

- to Steve and Kay for opening your home to help encourage this project along. May all that you do behind the scenes be rewarded to the glory of God's Kingdom!

- to Kenny for your thoughtfulness and dedication during the many hours of editing. Your insights helped the message of these pages to blossom. Your servant heart is a blessing helping others fulfill God's call on their life. In seeking God's Kingdom may your hand prosper and you find the multi-faceted riches of your inheritance!

A big "Thank you" to Sue Reidel for your wisdom and expertise throughout the entire book publishing process. You are an invaluable resource and prophetic voice. Your encouragement is much appreciated too! May the Lord's blessing cause you to flourish even greater in the days ahead!

Miracle Breakthroughs

FOREWORD
by Chuck Zimmer

There are several ways a father can shape his child's perspective and personhood. Many times, a father's relationship with his child will shape the mindset that a child has towards their Heavenly Father. Sara is our youngest child of four. By the time she came along, I had gained some experienced insight from Holy Spirit on how to point her in Abba Father's direction and encourage their intimacy to grow. Holy Spirit taught me to instill the reverential fear of the Lord and hatred of evil from the moment she was born (Proverbs 8:13, Proverbs 19:23). Using this revelation in raising and nurturing a child will guard their heart and develop their conscience.

Every person has a God-shaped void in their life which can only be filled through an intimate walk with their Creator. You can choose to fill that void with self-willed actions or to fill it with pure fellowship by building a relationship with the only Divine Love. Our desire for our daughter was that she would cultivate a level of intimacy with Abba that would guide and protect her throughout the fulfillment of her calling.

After Sara was brought home from the hospital, I held her on my shoulder and prayed into her being for the first 45 minutes in her new home. In my prayers, I released her to Father's loving care, sealed her divine destiny, and welcomed her to the family. I asked Abba for grace to develop her in her God-given will and purpose, and for the wisdom as a family to provide a safe haven for her growth. Essentially, I was giving her the confirmation of Father's love.

Miracle Breakthroughs

As she grew up, I taught her to desire to know God intimately, wait for Him to speak, and that His word was final. Her decisions were to be based on truth from the Bible. I also taught her that when she did make a mistake to quickly repent and run to Abba's arms for forgiveness. She was not to be ashamed of anything because Abba's love knows how to restore a repentant heart. It was important for her to know she needed to freely share her thoughts and decisions with Holy Spirit so that He could direct her path. Her transparency would be honored.

Whether or not you knew a Father's love growing up, I pray the words on these pages will release your soul to fellowship freely with an Abba whose love formed you and longs daily for warm intimate communion with you.

Abba's blessings,

Chuck Zimmer

(Proverbs 22:6)

A NOTE FROM THE AUTHOR

My parents always taught me of the importance of communing with Abba in all situations. If you lean on His wisdom and His loving arms, He will guide you down life's winding road. This book, Miracle Breakthroughs, was birthed from spiritual revelations, or "downloads from Heaven" as I like to call them, all of which were received during intimate times spent with the Lord. I began sharing some of these revelations with others, and found that they were benefitting from these truths as much as I was.

These pages represent Heaven's messages about everyday situations that either I or loved ones were encountering. Some of these downloads were clarification or redirection. Others were encouragement to build faith or stay the course. But no doubt about it, each of them were timely and accurate.

Holy Spirit was given to us to be our guide and help-mate in our daily lives. He will give you revelation into Abba's divine attributes and Kingdom plan if you ask Him. When we read God's Holy Word with a new understanding, it sparks a desire within us to know Abba in a more intimate way, and fellowship with Him and others according to His will. When we walk in the fruit of the Spirit, we flow with a holy ease and our communion is pure. When we flow in that communion, breakthrough follows.

As you seek to deepen your communion with Abba, I encourage you to ask Holy Spirit to reveal new insights into God's Holy Word. All of the resources of Heaven are ready to connect with you here on earth to bring about miracle breakthroughs. I pray that you will be strengthened with knowledge, wisdom, and understanding. May you be vulnerable

Miracle Breakthroughs

to your Heavenly Father and let Him minister to your needs and desires at all times. May your life be saturated with blessings. May each breakthrough ripple to those you encounter so the miracle of them all will bring many into God's glory. There is no testimony greater than one given because of God's love. There is no love like the love of your Abba!

With love,

Sara

- *Chapter One* -

Love

Miracle Breakthroughs

Love

DAY 1

M = Many
I = Incredible
R = Rapid
A = Accelerated
C = Cleansing
L = Leveling
E = Encounters

MIRACLES are manifesting soon or have already started to manifest in you and your family.

Behind every miracle, there is first compassion.

Jesus/Yeshua was moved with compassion and many encountered His loving touch and deliverance.

Let His love cleanse you and make you whole.

Let His miracles flow through you!

(Continued on next page...)

Miracle Breakthroughs

SCRIPTURE REFERENCE: **MARK 1:41-42 (NAS)**

Moved with compassion, Jesus stretched out His hand and touched him, and said to him, "I am willing; be cleansed." Immediately the leprosy left him and he was cleansed.

Love

DAY 2

SCRIPTURE REFERENCE: **PSALMS 46:10 (KJV)**

Be still, and know that I am God: I will be exalted among the heathen, I will be exalted in the earth.

SCRIPTURE REFERENCE: **1 JOHN 4:8 (KJV)**

He that loveth not knoweth not God, for God is love.

Be still and know that I am love.

Love creates an atmosphere of stillness.

Love cleanses Satan's deceptions of fear, shame, and separation.

When a person sins, it may not mean that they have a sin problem. Perhaps they haven't surrendered to the full embrace of God's love.

(Continued on next page...)

Miracle Breakthroughs

When we comprehend how fully we are loved, the desire to sin ceases to control us.

God truly is love. Period!

Go deeper in God. Go deeper in love.

Love

DAY 3

God's plans and purposes always start with love. They are kept with love and finish with love.

Transparency with Father God always begets a loving answer and comfort to every issue you may face.

May the depths of your soul cry out for God's measureless love.

His love is big enough to redeem every area of your life!

SCRIPTURE REFERENCE: **JEREMIAH 31:3-4 (NAS)**

The Lord appeared to him from afar, saying, "I have loved you with an everlasting love; therefore I have drawn you with lovingkindness. Again I will build you and you will be rebuilt, O virgin of Israel! Again you will take up your tambourines, and go forth to the dances of the merrymakers."

Love

DAY 4

God cares about the little things...

One evening, I dropped my dainty pearl earring. I quickly looked for it then said a prayer.

The following morning, while brushing my teeth, my foot stepped on something and there it was.

Thanks Abba!

How has Abba shown you lately that He loves you by tending to your little things?

SCRIPTURE REFERENCE: **LUKE 12:7 *(CJB)***

Why, every hair on your head has been counted! Don't be afraid, you are worth more than many sparrows.

Love

DAY 5

SCRIPTURE REFERENCE: **PSALMS 23:4 (NAS)**

Even though I walk through the valley of the shadow of death, I fear no evil, for You are with me; Your rod and Your staff, they comfort me.

Perfect love = no fear

When you know Abba's love, you have faith and trust in His protection and voice.

Walk on in the presence of His love! It will bring you to the other side of every valley.

Miracle Breakthroughs

Love

DAY 6

SCRIPTURE REFERENCE: **JOHN 3:16 (NAS)**

For God so loved the world, that He gave His only begotten Son, that whoever believes in Him shall not perish, but have eternal life.

L = Loving
O = Offer
V = Very
E = Extreme

The God of extreme love demonstrated great passion when He gave His only Son as a sacrifice for salvation, offering you abundant life, open access to fellowship with Abba, and the other benefits of salvation.

When we accept His offer of love and stay obedient, being overcome by the snares of the devil are no longer a concern.

May the intensity of His love surround you today and keep you for all eternity.

Love

DAY 7

SCRIPTURE REFERENCE: **PSALMS 119:114 (KJV)**

Thou art my hiding place and my shield: I hope in thy word.

When we are hidden away in our Savior, Jesus/Yeshua, His words are our shield.

His love is the foundation of each word.

We can trust in His every promise!

Love

DAY 8

*Scripture Reference: **Matthew 25:40 (NAS)***

The King will answer and say to them, Truly I say to you, to the extent that you did it to one of these brothers of Mine, even the least of them, you did it to Me.

Your love for Abba should be reflected in your daily actions. Let love be the guiding light of your thoughts and speech.

God's heart is touched in the same manner that you touch others.

May you hear His loving voice say, "Well done!", at the end of each day.

Love

DAY 9

SCRIPTURE REFERENCE: **PROVERBS 17:17 (NAS)**

A friend loves at all times...

Abba is our best friend: faithful, consistent, constant.

He has empowered us to imitate His characteristics!

Friendship and love go hand in hand.

Let us be Abba's hands and do the work of a friend.

Love

DAY 10

SCRIPTURE REFERENCE: LAMENTATIONS 3:22-23 (NAS)

The Lord's lovingkindnesses indeed never cease, for His compassions never fail. They are new every morning; great is Your faithfulness.

It should be a joy to wake up every morning, for each day is blessed with loving stability from Heaven!

Reflect on His lovingkindnesses!

Love

DAY 11

The love from the Lord is 100% natural... clean and pure!

We are to be imitators.

Love freely received is to be freely given.

SCRIPTURE REFERENCE: **MATTHEW 7:12 (MSG)**

Here is a simple, rule-of-thumb guide for behaviour: Ask yourself what you want people to do for you, then grab the initiative and do it for them. Add up God's Law and Prophets and this is what you get.

Love

DAY 12

SCRIPTURE REFERENCE: **PSALMS 12:6 (NAS)**

The words of the Lord are pure words; as silver tried in a furnace on the earth, refined seven times.

The number "seven" represents completion.

Today, may the fire of God's love purify your heart, bringing forth a matured love for one another.

May the fullness of seven reverberate through your being and permeate to those around you.

Be a walking seven of love!

Love

DAY 13

SCRIPTURE REFERENCE: **PSALMS 121:1 (KJV)**

I will lift up mine eyes unto the hills, from whence cometh my help.

Our help comes from Zion... from our Abba.

The court of Heaven convenes in Zion.

Jesus/Yeshua's blood and stripes are payment for the verdict.

Let the Cross be your reckoning place.

- For every sin, love answers
- For every verdict, love answers
- For every repentance, love answers

Fall into the arms of love and ask for what you need.

(Continued on next page...)

SCRIPTURE REFERENCE: **HEBREWS 4:16 (NAS)**

Therefore let us draw near with confidence to the throne of grace, so that we may receive mercy and find grace to help in time of need.

Love

DAY 14

I am so thankful that nothing catches God by surprise.

When we fully trust in Him, Abba's loving embrace makes steady and provides strength that we can rest in.

SCRIPTURE REFERENCE: **2 CHRONICLES 16:9 (NAS)**

For the eyes of the Lord move to and fro throughout the earth that He may strongly support those whose heart is completely His.

Love

DAY 15

Jesus... the King of Kings, Lord of Lords.

Jesus... the Bright Morning Star.

Jesus... the Forgiver of our sins.

Jesus... the Healer of our souls.

Jesus... our Bridegroom, whose love is impeccable.

Without Him, we are nothing. With Him, we are everything.

Jesus... your pleasantness empowers us to minister Your love, words, and healing to others!

SCRIPTURE REFERENCE: **SONG OF SOLOMON 1:16 (NAS)**

How handsome you are, my beloved, and so pleasant!

Love

DAY 16

Many times, we've been taught that we are to renew our mind and be transformed, at which point, we'd be victorious.

How about we take that truth one step further and ask for a transformation so we can lavishly love the Lord with all of our heart, soul, and strength?

Abba, we want to behold you and truly love you. We commune with You today and ask You to reveal how we can love You deeply.

May this day be marked as precious in Your sight.

SCRIPTURE REFERENCE: **LUKE 10:27 (NAS)**

And he answered, "You shall love the Lord your God with all your heart, and with all your soul, and with all your strength, and with all your mind; and your neighbor as yourself."

Love

DAY 17

Love sees the end from the beginning.

Our Abba saw the chasm that would need to be bridged to connect sinful man back to Himself. Jesus/Yeshua, the Passover Lamb, endured the cross and was resurrected to rejoin us with the Father.

Love and intimacy with Abba was the sustaining force that gave Jesus the strength to endure the suffering.

If you consider the Garden of Gethsemane and the amount of agony that Christ went through as He was sweating drops of blood, then you will see the demonstration of love and absolute commitment required to return man back to the loving arms of our loving Father.

Every act of love we do should reflect intimacy with Abba unto the end.

(Continued on next page...)

SCRIPTURE REFERENCE: **REVELATION 21:6 (NAS)**

I AM the Alpha and Omega, the Beginning and the End.

SCRIPTURE REFERENCE: **MATTHEW 26:38-39 (KJV)**

Then saith he unto them, My soul is exceeding sorrowful, even unto death: tarry ye here, and watch with me. And he went a little farther, and fell on his face, and prayed, saying, O my Father, if it be possible, let this cup pass from me: nevertheless not as I will, but as thou wilt.

Love

DAY 18

SCRIPTURE REFERENCE: **PROVERBS 10:22 (NAS)**

It is the blessing of the Lord that makes rich, and He adds no sorrow to it.

SCRIPTURE REFERENCE: **JAMES 1:17 (NAS)**

Every good thing given and every perfect gift is from above, coming down from the Father of lights, with whom there is no variation or shifting shadow.

How relaxing it is to dwell in the presence of God Almighty and know everything He gives is GOOD!

May you bask in the love of your Father today, knowing He is working good on your behalf.

Love

DAY 19

There are many different facets of love.

Love has no price tag.

Love, coupled with wisdom and justice, is powerful.

Love is strong. Love sets boundaries. Love forgives. Love heals. Love is like both a lion and a lamb.

Love is like a muscle... the more it is tried and worked, the stronger it becomes. This is how we rejoice in our trials and overcome.

Today, as your muscles are strengthened, may the love that has been shed abroad in your heart grow to perfected maturity.

SCRIPTURE REFERENCE: **PHILIPPIANS 1:6 (NAS)**

For I am confident of this very thing, that He who began a good work in you will perfect it until the day of Christ Jesus.

Love

DAY 20

SCRIPTURE REFERENCE: **HEBREWS 7:24-25 (NAS)**

But Jesus, on the other hand, because He continues forever, holds His priesthood permanently. Therefore He is able also to save forever those who draw near to God through Him, since He always lives to make intercession for them.

Through every season of my life, these verses have always touched my heart deeply and surrounded me tenderly.

To believe that Jesus/Yeshua is in Heaven interceding for our good should strengthen our faith to overcome.

With His support behind you, all things are possible!

Let this great love bring peace to your daily activities.

Love

DAY 21

SCRIPTURE REFERENCE: **PSALMS 92:1-2 (KJV)**

It is a good thing to give thanks unto the Lord, and to sing praises unto thy name, O most High: To show forth thy lovingkindness in the morning, and thy faithfulness every night.

God is faithful during your sleep and meets you with great kindness upon your waking. He will light your steps with His word. Goodness and mercy will follow you everywhere you go.

Jesus/Yeshua longs to show forth His love to you the whole day through!

Today is filled with the promise of "yes and amen". Let everything you say and do permeate the atmosphere with Kingdom purpose.

Love

DAY 22

Flexible means being capable of bending easily without breaking.

Yielding to God's nature and the sound of Heaven is beautiful in His sight. He longs to saturate every part of your being.

Let God take every "stiff" area in your life, soften them up, and turn you loose to shine His love to the hurting.

Now there is a testimony!

SCRIPTURE REFERENCE: **EZEKIEL 11:19-20 (KJV)**

And I will give them one heart, and put a new spirit within them. And I will take the heart of stone out of their flesh and give them a heart of flesh, that they may walk in My statutes and keep My ordinances and do them. Then they will be My people, and I shall be their God.

Love

DAY 23

"Making melody in our hearts unto the King of Kings..."

Remember that song? If a light shines on your heart, would the ingredients for a melodious recipe be found? Love, joy, goodness, mercy, kindness, etc. or envy, competition, judgment, contention, etc.

If we want to taste and see that the Lord is good, we need to be mixing the correct ingredients!

SCRIPTURE REFERENCE: **PHILIPPIANS 4:8 (NAS)**

Finally, brethren, whatever is true, whatever is honorable, whatever is right, whatever is pure, whatever is lovely, whatever is of good repute, if there is any excellence and if anything worthy of praise, dwell on these things.

Love

DAY 24

SCRIPTURE REFERENCE: *JOHN 15:9 (KJV)*

As the Father hath loved me, so have I loved you: continue ye in my love.

The beginning is love. The middle is love. The end is love. Love is what created us and sustains us.

Love is the most powerful force behind every thought, word, and deed.

Love sees us for who we are. It looks past the external to what lies beneath. Love never gives up on others.

Love always triumphs!

Let the love in your eyes see the good in others...face to face...heart to heart. We were created to love.

Love

DAY 25

SCRIPTURE REFERENCE: **PSALMS 11:7 (NAS)**

For the Lord is righteous, He loves righteousness; the upright will behold His face.

If God is righteous, and we are made in His image and walk in His ways, then so are we.

If God loves righteousness, so He loves us.

Expect to see His face today!

Love

DAY 26

Jesus/Yeshua is the light of the world.

If Jesus lives in us, we should shine too!

The greatest way to shine is to love!

Jesus shines this verse impeccably...

SCRIPTURE REFERENCE: **JOHN 15:13 (NAS)**

No one has greater love than a person who lays down his life for his friends.

Jesus laid down his mind, will, and emotions for His friends.

Be His light and shine His example!

Love

DAY 27

The greatest thing in all my life is...
- Loving you, Lord
- Knowing you, Lord
- Fellowshipping with you, Lord
- Being in your presence, Lord
- Doing your will, Lord
- And most of all, being your friend, Lord!

I pray that our hunger and our will be towards the One we love, pressing to reach to a greater depth in obedience.

This depth in obedience is where life begins and is sustained... so simple, yet so pure.

SCRIPTURE REFERENCE: **ISAIAH 58:8 (NAS)**

Then your light will break out like the dawn, and your recovery will speedily spring forth; and your righteousness will go before you; the glory of the Lord will be your rear guard.

Love

DAY 28

God is love...PERIOD!

God lives inside us. We should love greater than others can hurt us.

Love is a non-stick coating. Loving forgiveness is true victory.

People test the love light. When they find it to be real, what sweet answers they find!

Let your love light shine today. It could very well bring the deliverance for another soul.

SCRIPTURE REFERENCE: **MATTHEW 5:16 (NAS)**

Let your light shine before men in such a way that they may see your good works, and glorify your Father who is in heaven.

Love

DAY 29

When I think of Jesus/Yeshua, I think about His love and character. I think more about who He is, rather than what He did.

What do you want your legacy to be?

Let the fruit of the Spirit shine through your actions.

Will people remember you more for how you love and uplift them than the great things you accomplish?

SCRIPTURE REFERENCE: **PROVERBS 22:1 (NAS)**

A good name is rather to be chosen than great riches, and loving favor rather than silver and gold.

Love

DAY 30

When the truth is known, compassion should follow.

Jesus/Yeshua is our example. How many times does The Bible say that He was moved with compassion? Many!

The results...many miracles followed and changed people forever!

I pray that a double portion of compassion grow in you from the inside out. Go forth as a compassionate blessing!

SCRIPTURE REFERENCE: **MATTHEW 20:34 (NAS)**

Moved with compassion, Jesus touched their eyes; and immediately they regained their sight and followed Him.

Love

DAY 31

SCRIPTURE REFERENCE: *I JOHN 4:18-19 (NAS)*

There is no fear in love; but perfect love casts out fear, because fear involves punishment, and the one who fears is not perfected in love. We love, because He first loved us.

Oh, how Abba loves us!

All his ways are good.

Rest in His love and soar.

Give His love away and live...

Selah!

- *Chapter Two* -

Peace

Miracle Breakthroughs

Peace

DAY 1

M = Many
I = Incredible
R = Rapid
A = Accelerated
C = Cleansing
L = Leveling
E = Encounters

Did you know that shalom means "nothing broken, nothing missing" in Hebrew?

The state of shalom is one of peace and contentment.

Shalom can also be interpreted as the peace created when you trust that Father God makes all things work together for the good of those who love Him.

God is bringing forth many miracles to set us in a place of shalom!

(Continued on next page...)

Miracle Breakthroughs

Scripture Reference: **Psalms 122:8 (CJB)**

For the sake of my family and friends, I say, "Shalom be within you!"

Scripture Reference: **Romans 8:28 (KJV)**

And we know that all things work together for good to them that love God, to them who are the called according to his purpose.

Peace

DAY 2

SCRIPTURE REFERENCE: *ISAIAH 9:6-7 (KJV)*

For unto us a child is born, unto us a son is given: and the government shall be upon His shoulder: and His name shall be called Wonderful, Counsellor, the Mighty God, the Everlasting Father, the Prince of Peace. Of the increase of His government and peace there shall be no end, upon the throne of David, and upon His kingdom, to order it, and to establish it with judgment and with justice from henceforth even for ever. The zeal of the Lord of Hosts will perform this.

The Prince of Peace is reigning today and forever. His judgment and justice are pure.

Declare the reigning of the Prince of Peace over every area of your life, and proclaim His Kingdom in our land. He is our friend. Let His love be shed abroad in our hearts so all can be brought into peaceful order.

Peace

DAY 3

SCRIPTURE REFERENCE: ISAIAH 32:16-17 (NAS)

Then justice will dwell in the wilderness and righteousness will abide in the fertile field. And the work of righteousness will be peace, and the service of righteousness, quietness and confidence forever.

The foundation of God's throne is righteousness and justice, which yields peace.

As you go about your day, keep your eyes open to see God's righteousness and justice working to bring peaceful quietness and confidence into every circumstance and situation in your life.

Lord, open our eyes to recognize your fingers weaving a tapestry of peace!

Peace

DAY 4

SCRIPTURE REFERENCE: **I CHRONICLES 16:31 (NAS)**

Let the heavens be glad, and let the earth rejoice; and let them say among the nations, the Lord reigns.

SCRIPTURE REFERENCE: **PSALMS 118:24 (NAS)**

This is the day which the Lord has made; let us rejoice and be glad in it.

Rejoice in the Lord! Why? Because...

SCRIPTURE REFERENCE: **EXODUS 14:14 (KJV)**

The Lord shall fight for you, and you shall hold your peace.

Keep your "rejoicer" active and peace will steady your day!

Peace

DAY 5

SCRIPTURE REFERENCE: **ROMANS 14:16-19 (NAS)**

Therefore do not let what is for you a good thing be spoken of as evil; for the kingdom of God is [...] righteousness and peace and joy in the Holy Spirit. For he who in this way serves Christ is acceptable to God and approved by men. So then we pursue the things which make for peace and the building up of one another.

Seek first the Kingdom of God... righteousness, peace and joy.

When you seek His Kingdom, you will walk in righteousness, peace, and joy, because they are found in His presence.

When we stay in His presence, it brings peace, and the words that we speak will naturally edify one another.

Peace

DAY 6

SCRIPTURE REFERENCE: **ROMANS 8:6 (NAS)**

For the mind set on the flesh is death, but the mind set on the Spirit is life and peace.

The Spirit life is peace.

The Spirit mind is peace.

When we take on a mind renewed by the Holy Spirit, we can rest in a peace that passes understanding.

May the peace of God abiding in you continually deliver Heaven on Earth into your "now".

Let God's peace bring healing and quiet assurance to your world today... that all may see and rejoice in the Spirit of the Lord.

Pass along peace!

Peace

DAY 7

May peace renew your soul and revive you for the days ahead.

Hear the Spirit inviting us to, "Come away my Beloved, rest in me and find peace."

Obey the Lord's instructions and you will have peace... therein lies the blessing.

SCRIPTURE REFERENCE: **NUMBERS 6:24-26 (KJV)**

The Lord bless thee, and keep thee: the Lord make his face shine upon thee, and be gracious unto thee: the Lord lift up his countenance upon thee, and give thee peace.

Peace

DAY 8

There is peace in the eye of a hurricane. In peace, there is rest.

SCRIPTURE REFERENCE: **ISAIAH 26:3 (NAS)**

The steadfast of mind You will keep in perfect peace, because he trusts in You.

There is a fight to stay at rest.

Decide today to resist the distractions of life's storms and center your soul in the eye of peace.

Peace

DAY 9

Resting brings healing...

Worrying is the opposite of rest.

Give your soul permission to rest today.

Move into rest. Move into peace.

SCRIPTURE REFERENCE: **PSALMS 62:5 (KJV)**

My soul, wait thou only upon God; for my expectation is from him.

Peace

DAY 10

There is a dwelling place of quiet rest, joy, and contentment in the presence of God.

There is a place of unending peace deep in the heart of God.

Stay there... rest there... experience the joy there.

SCRIPTURE REFERENCE: **ISAIAH 14:7 (NAS)**

The whole earth is at rest and is quiet; they break forth into shouts of joy.

Peace

DAY 11

Life is so exciting when you wait on the Lord instead of charging ahead, trying to make it happen in your own strength.

Let Abba's love be the rhythm of your heart.

His timing brings peaceful rest and makes beautiful.

SCRIPTURE REFERENCE: **PSALMS 16:5-6 (NAS)**

The Lord is the portion of my inheritance and my cup; you support my lot. The lines have fallen to me in pleasant places; indeed, my heritage is beautiful to me.

Peace

DAY 12

I woke up this morning thinking about the names of God... Abba, Yahweh, I Am...

Then on to Jesus... Prince of Peace, Rose of Sharon, Yeshua

Then on to Holy Spirit... Ruach HaKodesh, Comforter, Guide

Doesn't your heart warm when you say the name of someone you love and think about their attributes?

Oh, how I love Father, Son, and Holy Spirit!

My heart is now at peace and ready for this day.

SCRIPTURE REFERENCE: *ISAIAH* **26:3 (KJV)**

Thou wilt keep him in perfect peace, whose mind is stayed on thee: because he trusteth in thee.

Peace

DAY 13

SCRIPTURE REFERENCE: **EPHESIANS 4:1-3 (NAS)**

Therefore I, the prisoner of the Lord, implore you to walk in a manner worthy of the calling with which you have been called, with all humility and gentleness, with patience, showing tolerance for one another in love, being diligent to preserve the unity of the Spirit in the bond of peace.

Let the eye of the Lord guide you into all truth.

Let the walk of His calling come alive in you, saturating your being, your thoughts, and your actions.

Let the mind of Christ be in you.

Become an instrument of peace...chords of compassion your song.

Peace

DAY 14

SCRIPTURE REFERENCE: **JOB 22:21-22 (NAS)**

Yield now and be at peace with Him; thereby good will come to you. Please receive instruction from His mouth and establish His words in your heart.

SCRIPTURE REFERENCE: **ROMANS 8:28 (KJV)**

And we know that all things work together for good to them that love God, to them who are the called according to his purpose.

When you are fully submitted to God's purpose, you are not wresting against His will.

When you are not wrestling against His will, your soul is at peace. You know that He is working all things for your good and you are content with the outcome.

Peace

DAY 15

SCRIPTURE REFERENCE: **2 THESSALONIANS 3:16 (CJB)**

Now may the Lord of shalom himself give you shalom always in all ways. The Lord be with all of you.

Earlier, we learned that shalom means "nothing broken, nothing missing".

Shalom always...

God is constantly transforming our lives. He takes the fragmented parts of our souls, healing them into "nothing broken". He bestows blessings running over, filling us so our hearts can proclaim, "nothing missing".

He sees the end from the present. Rest in the peace from trusting that His completed work in your life begets perfect shalom always.

Peace

DAY 16

SCRIPTURE REFERENCE: **MATTHEW 11:28-30 (NAS)**

Come to Me, all who are weary and heavy-laden, and I will give you rest. Take My yoke upon you and learn from Me, for I am gentle and humble in heart, and you will find rest for your souls. For My yoke is easy and My burden is light.

One of my favorite words contained in these verses is "come". To be invited by someone means that they care and truly want you.

Today, Holy Spirit is wooing you with gentleness, peace, and humility to rest in Father's loving care.

Abba has it all in the palm of His hands!

Simply put, He wants us to relax and be at peace while He calls the shots.

Peace

DAY 17

In the midst of great darkness, light shines.

In the midst of great tragedy, love heals.

In the midst of what is hidden, truth reveals.

Let peace illuminate your everyday life and radiate wholeness.

SCRIPTURE REFERENCE: **LUKE 11:36 (NAS)**

If therefore your whole body is full of light, with no dark part in it, it will be wholly illumined, as when the lamp illumines you with its rays.

Peace

DAY 18

"Carry on my wayward son. There will be peace when you are done." The words to that song are full of meaning and spark many thoughts. Remember the parable of the prodigal and his brother. Both siblings were living their lives based on their own ideals. When we stop functioning in our own strength or will (regardless of good intentions or bad decisions) and yield to Father's divine plans, we will operate in perfected peace.

Abba's arms are full of comfort, always inviting and ever responding.

Abba has His eye on every person. His heart yearns for their nearness.

Open our eyes Lord, let us see others as you see them. Bring us into your warm embrace. Make us unified in your family!

(Continued on next page...)

Miracle Breakthroughs

SCRIPTURE REFERENCE: **MATTHEW 18:12-14 (NAS)**

What do you think? If any man has a hundred sheep, and one of them has gone astray, does he not leave the ninety-nine on the mountains and go and search for the one that is straying? If it turns out that he finds it, truly I say to you, he rejoices over it more than over the ninety-nine which have not gone astray. So it is not the will of your Father who is in heaven that one of these little ones perish.

SCRIPTURE REFERENCE: **LUKE 15:28-32 (MSG)**

The older brother stalked off in an angry sulk and refused to join in. His father came out and tried to talk to him, but he wouldn't listen. The son said, "Look how many years I've stayed here serving you, never giving you one moment of grief, but have you ever thrown a party for me and my friends? Then this son of yours who has thrown away your money on whores shows up and you go all out with a feast!"

His father said, "Son, you don't understand. You're with me all the time, and everything that is mine is yours—but this is a wonderful time, and we had to celebrate. This brother of yours was dead, and he's alive! He was lost, and he's found!"

Peace

DAY 19

SCRIPTURE REFERENCE: **COLOSSIANS 3:15 (NAS)**

Let the peace of Christ rule in your hearts, to which indeed you were called in one body; and be thankful.

Peace brings unity.

Peace keeps alignment.

When there is peace, unity, and alignment, there is **much** to be thankful for.

Let peace have high reign in your heart!

Peace

DAY 20

SCRIPTURE REFERENCE: *ZECHARIAH 8:16 (NAS)*

These are the things which you should do: speak the truth to one another; judge with truth and judgment for peace in your gates.

Speak truth that heals.

Speak truth that divides good and evil.

Speak truth that opens the gates to repentance.

Speak truth that draws the children to the Father.

Where there is truth received, peace abounds!

Peace

DAY 21

We will be at peace, Abba, while we pray and praise you.

You will take the fruit of our actions and fight the battle for us.

We see VICTORY!

SCRIPTURE REFERENCE: **EXODUS 14:13-14 (KJV)**

And Moses said unto the people, Fear ye not, stand still, and see the salvation of the Lord, which he will shew to you today: for the Egyptians whom ye have seen today, ye shall see them again no more for ever. The Lord shall fight for you, and ye shall hold your peace.

Peace

DAY 22

SCRIPTURE REFERENCE: **MATTHEW 5:8-9 (KJV)**

Blessed are the pure in heart, for they shall see God. Blessed are the peacemakers, for they shall be called sons of God.

When we see and know God, we can bring reconciliation...becoming peacemakers between human souls and God.

That is a pure transaction between Heaven and Earth.

Peace

DAY 23

Saying "YES" to what God says yes to and "NO" to what God says no to brings shalom (peace).

...nothing broken, nothing missing in God's time.

SCRIPTURE REFERENCE: **PROVERBS 3:5-8 (CJB)**

Trust in ADONAI with all your heart; do not rely on your own understanding. In all your ways acknowledge him; then he will level your paths. Don't be conceited about your own wisdom; but fear ADONAI, and turn from evil. This will bring health to your body and give strength to your bones.

Peace

DAY 24

Live in peace.

Rest in peace.

God's eye watches your every breath. He will move you forward on the true path when you trust His word.

SCRIPTURE REFERENCE: **PSALMS 32:8 (NAS)**

I will instruct you and teach you in the way which you should go; I will counsel you with my eye upon you.

SCRIPTURE REFERENCE: **PSALMS 23:3 (MSG)**

True to your word, you let me catch my breath and send me in the right direction.

Peace

DAY 25

Our Heavenly Father cares enough about us that he wants us to dwell in peaceful surroundings.

Speak peace to whatever troubled waters come your way and believe and they will be stilled.

May your day be filled with blessed, peaceful stillness.

SCRIPTURE REFERENCE: **PSALMS 23:1-2 (NLT)**

The Lord is my shepherd; I have everything I need. He lets me rest in green meadows; he leads me beside peaceful streams.

Peace

DAY 26

Sweet Peace...
Bountiful Peace...
Graceful Peace...

When you are a reflection of Jesus/Yeshua, the Prince of Peace, you will naturally radiate peace and harmony to others. When you work in harmony, there is no discord.

Seek God's face and let His countenance light the world around you.

I'm praying that the fruit of your fellowship with the Prince of Peace would shine so brightly that others will be drawn to the Source of Light.

SCRIPTURE REFERENCE: **NUMBERS 26:6 (NAS)**

The Lord lift up His countenance on you, and give you peace.

Peace

DAY 27

When you are perfectly aligned with the King, there can be complete chaos all around, but great peace reigning inside you.

Selah!

SCRIPTURE REFERENCE: *JOHN 14:26-27 (NAS)*

But the Helper, the Holy Spirit, whom the Father will send in My name, He will teach you all things, and bring to your remembrance all that I said to you. Peace I leave with you; my peace I give to you; not as the world gives do I give to you. Do not let your heart be troubled, nor let it be fearful.

Peace

DAY 28

SCRIPTURE REFERENCE: JOSHUA 1:9 (KJV)

Have not I commanded thee? Be strong and of a good courage; be not afraid, neither be thou dismayed: for the Lord thy God is with thee whithersoever thou goest.

Keeping our focus on the Lord brings strength, courage, and peace.

Moment by moment...

Day by day...

Each step you take will be sure.

Peace

DAY 29

SCRIPTURE REFERENCE: **NUMBERS 13:30 (NAS)**

Then Caleb quieted the people before Moses and said, "We should by all means go up and take possession of it, for we will surely overcome it."

Whatever we possess, we overcome.

When we take captive every thought that goes against God's word, we overcome.

Today, let us set our will to possess the promised land of our mind and conquer the giants that are contrary to God's peace.

Let God's Kingdom of righteousness, peace, and joy be upon us and flow out of us!

Possess and overcome!

Peace

DAY 30

In the middle of a hurricane there is always an eye of peace.

Abba, give us vision to see the eye, your divine place of peaceful refuge. Give us grace to dwell with You, and the peace to meditate in Your holy place.

SCRIPTURE REFERENCE: **PSALMS 27:4 (NAS)**

One thing I have asked from the Lord, that I shall seek: that I may dwell in the house of the Lord all the days of my life, to behold the beauty of the Lord and to meditate in His temple.

Peace

DAY 31

Scripture Reference: **Song of Solomon 6:13 (MSG)**

Dance, dance, dear Shulammite, Angel-Princess! Dance, and we'll feast our eyes on your grace! Everyone wants to see the Shulammite dance her victory dances of love and peace.

Scripture Reference: **Revelation 21:2 (KJV)**

And I John saw the holy city, new Jerusalem, coming down from God out of heaven, prepared as a bride adorned for her husband.

Let the world feast their eyes on the movement of the Prince of Peace with His Bride!

May God's glory light your being with the grace to dance in the peace of the Bridegroom's arms.

Selah!

- *Chapter Three* -

Joyous Praise

Miracle Breakthroughs

Joyous Praise

DAY 1

M = Many
I = Incredible
R = Rapid
A = Accelerated
C = Cleansing
L = Leveling
E = Encounters

The Lord takes great pleasure from the praise that erupts from our mouth as Abba's mighty hand moves mountains and makes our enemies powerless.

He is worthy of our exuberant praise!

SCRIPTURE REFERENCE: **PSALMS 149:4-6 (KJV)**

For the Lord taketh pleasure in his people: he will beautify the meek with salvation. Let the saints be joyful in glory: let them sing aloud upon their beds. Let the high praises of God be in their mouth, and a two-edged sword in their hand;

Joyous Praise

DAY 2

When you delight in God's unwavering righteousness, you will have great peace.

The overflow from your heart is uncontainable praise to Adonai.

Purpose in your heart to dwell on your divinely-orchestrated right standing with Abba, and the flow of joyous praise will come naturally.

SCRIPTURE REFERENCE: **PSALMS 35:27 (CJB)**

But may those who delight in my righteousness shout for joy and be glad! Let them say always, "How great is ADONAI, who delights in the peace of his servant!" Then my tongue will tell of your righteousness and praise you all day long.

Joyous Praise

DAY 3

What a beautiful morning!

Embrace the new mercies, which His Spirit pours out at your waking.

Today is a day of rejoicing! Hear the shouts of joy as Adonai rejoices over you, His child.

Savor His salvation. He is with you every moment of every day.

Release your heart to live in the Sonshine!

SCRIPTURE REFERENCE: **ZEPHANIAH 3:17 (CJB)**

ADONAI your God is right there with you, as a mighty savior. He will rejoice over you and be glad, he will be silent in his love, he will shout over you with joy.

Joyous Praise

DAY 4

Scripture Reference: **Psalms 126:1-2 (KJV)**

When the Lord turned again the captivity of Zion, we were like them that dream. Then was our mouth filled with laughter, and our tongue with singing: then said they among the heathen, the Lord hath done great things for them.

Dream!

Dream again!

Laugh again!

Rejoice again!

Believe and rejoice that the Lord is doing great things!

Your captivity is over. Rejoice!

Joyous Praise

DAY 5

When you know your Abba, His salvation makes you strong.

When you know your Abba, praise is natural.

Be strong and sing!

Great is our God!

SCRIPTURE REFERENCE: *EXODUS 15:2 (NAS)*

The Lord is my strength and song, and He has become my salvation; this is my God, and I will praise Him; my father's God, and I will extol Him.

Joyous Praise

DAY 6

SCRIPTURE REFERENCE: **REVELATION 14:7 (NAS)**

and he said with a loud voice, "Fear God, and give Him glory, because the hour of His judgment has come; worship Him who made the heaven and the earth and sea and springs of waters."

Judgment brings justice.

Justice corrects the wrongs into rights.

Rejoice and give thanks for judgment!

Joyous Praise

DAY 7

Abba, You are the greatest of all! We lift up our prayers to you, and leave them in your big hands as we go our way rejoicing.

You delight to show Your splendor of making the impossible possible!

Abba, there is none like You!

SCRIPTURE REFERENCE: **PSALMS 19:1 (NAS)**

The heavens are telling of the glory of God; and their expanse is declaring the work of His hands.

Joyous Praise

DAY 8

SCRIPTURE REFERENCE: *ISAIAH 55:9-12 (NAS)*

For as the heavens are higher than the earth, so are my ways higher than your ways, and my thoughts than your thoughts. For as the rain cometh down, and the snow from heaven, and returneth not thither, but watereth the earth, and maketh it bring forth and bud, that it may give seed to the sower, and bread to the eater: So will my word be which goes forth from my mouth; it will not return to me empty, without accomplishing what I desire, and without succeeding in the matter for which I sent it. For you will go out with joy and be led forth with peace; the mountains and the hills will break forth into shouts of joy before you, and all the trees of the field will clap their hands.

The Lord reigns...His thoughts and ways are high!

The Lord reigns...let the earth, the hills, and the trees rejoice!

(Continued on next page...)

The Lord reigns...His words always accomplish their intended purpose!

Hunger to know His thoughts and ways.

Hunger for Him deeply and He will be your everything!

Rejoice for your Abba is Alpha and Omega!

Joyous Praise

DAY 9

Looking for a reason to rejoice today? Luke 15 has a great answer...

SCRIPTURE REFERENCE: **LUKE 15:7 (NAS)**

I tell you that in the same way, there will be more joy in heaven over one sinner who repents than over ninety-nine righteous persons who need no repentance.

The Holy Spirit, hosts of angels, and all of Heaven's resources are working with us today to bring redemption to a soul.

Let's keep our eyes open for the "one" we are to minister to and bring Heaven to Earth!

Heaven is always ready to rejoice with us!

Joyous Praise

DAY 10

Where there is truth there is great joy!

Where there is truth there is great strength!

The joy of the Lord is your strength!

Abba smiles when truth prevails.

Let your testimony of truth be offered up as joyful praise unto Abba.

SCRIPTURE REFERENCE: **3 JOHN 1:3-4 (NAS)**

For I was very glad when brethren came and testified to your truth, that is, how you are walking in truth. I have no greater joy than this, to hear of my children walking in the truth.

Joyous Praise

DAY 11

SCRIPTURE REFERENCE: *I CHRONICLES 16:29-30 (KJV)*

Give unto the Lord the glory due unto his name: bring an offering, and come before him: worship the Lord in the beauty of holiness. Fear before him, all the earth: the world also shall be stable, that it be not moved.

There is great beauty in worshiping with purity (holiness) and living in the reverential fear of our Lord. Holy worship brings stability to your soul, and soothes it so that you will not be moved by circumstance.

Alignment with Heaven comes as we glorify our King, offering up the sacrifice of worship. Worship is not a formula or works. It is beautiful praise, freely flowing from a pure heart of innocence to bring pleasure to our adoring Abba.

Let it be your delight to exuberantly address your praises upward so all you see is the pleasure radiating from Father's face.

Joyous Praise

DAY 12

SCRIPTURE REFERENCE: *ISAIAH 35:10 (NAS)*

And the ransomed of the Lord will return and come with joyful shouting to Zion, with everlasting joy upon their heads. They will find gladness and joy, and sorrow and sighing will flee away.

The King is reigning from Zion. Let us find gladness and joy, and shout our way to the heart of Zion.

Sorrows and burdens cannot exist in the same space as gladness and joy. Therefore, let us cast off sorrows and burdens with our exuberant praise unto Abba, for we are in His heart!

This promise is cause for great rejoicing!

Joyous Praise

DAY 13

SCRIPTURE REFERENCE: **PSALMS 57:8-11 (NAS)**

Awake, my glory! Awake, harp and lyre! I will awaken the dawn. I will give thanks to You, O Lord, among the peoples; I will sing praises to You among the nations. For Your lovingkindness is great to the heavens and Your truth to the clouds. Be exalted above the heavens, O God; let Your glory be above all the earth.

When you start your day with praises emanating from your lips, you usher in the Father's glory into your surroundings.

With that in mind...awaken and give thanks!

Sing praise and exalt!

Receive truth and behold the glory!

These are our marching orders. Let's praise together!

Joyous Praise

DAY 14

SCRIPTURE REFERENCE: **JEREMIAH 31:13 (NAS)**

Then the virgin will rejoice in the dance, and the young men and the old, together, for I will turn their mourning into joy and will comfort them and give them joy for their sorrow.

When we look at circumstances with natural eyes, it is easy to see distress and hopelessness in the world. However, looking with spiritual eyes, we see the bigger picture, and understand that Jehovah is the God of turnaround and alignment!

When there is turnaround there is much cause for dancing and joyful praise! With correction and recalibration, the plans of the enemy are rendered ineffective. Therefore, dance and praise to usher in joy, for your dance is crushing the head of the enemy!

Let your comfort be found in the joy of the Lord!

Joyous Praise

DAY 15

SCRIPTURE REFERENCE: **2 SAMUEL 6:14-15 (KJV)**

And David danced before the Lord with all his might; and David was girded with a linen ephod. So David and all the house of Israel brought up the ark of the Lord with shouting, and with the sound of the trumpet.

There is pure excitement to be in the presence of the Lord, and to become as an innocent child before Him, praising with all your might.

Long for the joy, the delight, and the knowing of deeper intimacy with Jesus/Yeshua. Let us ask God for fresh yearning, awe, and delight as we bask and dance with Him, in His presence.

Joyous Praise

DAY 16

SCRIPTURE REFERENCE: **PSALMS 32:11 (NAS)**

Be glad in the Lord and rejoice, you righteous ones; and shout for joy, all you who are upright in heart.

Abba encourages us to rejoice and be full of joy as our praises shout out from an upright heart.

Rejoice! The Lord reigns.

Rejoice! Heaven and Earth have kissed.

Rejoice! God is NOT dead. He's truly alive!

Rejoice! All of creation is cleansing.

Rejoice! The Bride is making herself ready.

SCRIPTURE REFERENCE: **PHILIPPIANS 4:4 (KJV)**

Rejoice in the Lord always: and again I say, Rejoice.

Joyous Praise

DAY 17

Let your shouts of joy bring forth a new song!

As your joy raises to higher levels, do not stifle the song that erupts from your heart.

The best music comes forth from the purest of praise.

Have a joy-filled day!

SCRIPTURE REFERENCE: **PSALMS 33:3 (CJB)**

Sing to him a new song, make music at your best among shouts of joy.

Joyous Praise

DAY 18

My Jesus/Yeshua, You are near and dear to me.

It is so easy to give You praise, my Love.

My heart sings as You tell me Your commandments.

Your praises on my lips will inspire me to carry forth your instructions.

Teach me, my Adonai!

SCRIPTURE REFERENCE: **PSALMS 119:171 (NAS)**

Let my lips utter praise, for You teach me Your statutes.

Joyous Praise

DAY 19

Today is a day to arise and shine and praise the Lord!

Let your voice ring out with rapturous praise and prayer.

Bask in the Lord and anticipate His goodness to order your day.

Keep your eyes open wide. Answers are on the way.

SCRIPTURE REFERENCE: **PSALMS 5:3 (NAS)**

In the morning, O LORD, You will hear my voice; in the morning I will order my prayer to You and eagerly watch.

Joyous Praise

DAY 20

SCRIPTURE REFERENCE: **ISAIAH 56:7 (NAS)**

Even those I will bring to My holy mountain and make them joyful in My house of prayer. Their burnt offerings and their sacrifices will be acceptable on My altar; for My house will be called a house of prayer for all the peoples.

Rejoice, children of the Most High, for your Father has made a way for His people of all nations to commune with Him equally.

Come into His presence joyfully and worship Him. He loves to delight in the praises of His children.

Your sacrifices of praise and thanksgiving will not be ignored, as they are a sweet aroma in the nostrils of Adonai.

May the holy mount reverberate with your praise today as you give glory from your temple, where He abides.

Joyous Praise

DAY 21

God inhabits your praise.

Is there an area of your life where you need breakthrough?

Well, turn up the praise and let God happen!

Let the praise go up and watch the walls come down.

Let the praise go up and watch the prison doors open for freedom and breakthrough!

SCRIPTURE REFERENCE: **PSALMS 22:3-4 (NAS)**

Yet You are holy, O You who are enthroned upon the praises of Israel. In You our fathers trusted; they trusted and You delivered them.

Joyous Praise

DAY 22

SCRIPTURE REFERENCE: *I CHRONICLES 16:8-10 (CJB)*

Give thanks to ADONAI! Call on His name! Make His deeds known among the peoples. Sing to Him, sing praises to Him! Talk about all His wonders. Glory in His holy name; let those seeking ADONAI have joyful hearts.

If you are looking for joy, this scripture has an answer for you. Seek and praise Adonai!

Let our thoughts and words permeate the atmosphere with faith, bringing the awesomeness of God's presence into manifestation.

Expect glorious signs and wonders to confirm God's words!

Joyous Praise

DAY 23

SCRIPTURE REFERENCE: **PROVERBS 17:22 (KJV)**

A merry heart doeth good like a medicine...

A merry heart is God's antidote to trouble and care.

Praise on your lips yields healing for your being.

May your day be filled with joyful moments of healing and laughter.

Have a joyful praise eruption!

Joyous Praise

DAY 24

SCRIPTURE REFERENCE: **PSALM 141:2 (CJB)**

Let my prayer be like incense set before you, my uplifted hands like an evening sacrifice.

Our words, thoughts, and actions are charged with meaning. God places great weight on the intent of our heart. We should be as conscious of our daily deeds as Father is, for they are sacred.

Purpose that your sacrificial praise be holy, acceptable, and pleasing unto Abba. Desire that the incense of your deeds and prayers be a sweet smelling aroma in His nostrils.

Joyous Praise

DAY 25

Let the lightness of the Spirit fall on you! It is the grace for smooth movement. Let it turn you, whirl you, pick you up, and put your feet back down on lush green pastures.

Let joyous praises spring forth from your heart!

SCRIPTURE REFERENCE: **PSALM 23 (KJV)**

The Lord is my shepherd; I shall not want. He maketh me to lie down in green pastures: he leadeth me beside the still waters. He restoreth my soul: he leadeth me in the paths of righteousness for his name's sake. Yea, though I walk through the valley of the shadow of death, I will fear no evil: for thou art with me; thy rod and thy staff they comfort me. Thou preparest a table before me in the presence of mine enemies: thou anointest my head with oil; my cup runneth over. Surely goodness and mercy shall follow me all the days of my life: and I will dwell in the house of the Lord for ever.

Joyous Praise

DAY 26

SCRIPTURE REFERENCE: **PSALMS 30:11-12 (CJB)**

You turned my mourning into dancing! You removed my sackcloth and clothed me with joy, so that my well-being can praise you and not be silent; ADONAI my God, I will thank you forever!

A joyful testimony infuses the atmosphere with praise and thanksgiving!

I'm excited for all the glorious turning that Abba is working now and the testimonies that will be released as a result of His goodness.

Adonai delights to see His beloved children joyful and prosperous.

Erupt forth in glorious praise!

Joyous Praise

DAY 27

We rejoice in You, oh Lord, for you have made this day delightful! Our hearts are overjoyed with gladness from the works of your mighty hand. As You order our day, we will be mindful to give You praise and thanksgiving in all that we say and do. Your very name is holy, and we call on it now to manifest Heaven into our midst. We just want to be where you are, Abba. Have your way, Holy Spirit, and may Father God be glorified from all nations and people. For thine is the kingdom, and the power, and the glory, for ever. Amen.

SCRIPTURE REFERENCE: **PSALMS 100:4 (KJV)**

Enter into His gates with thanksgiving, and into His courts with praise: be thankful unto Him, and bless His name.

Joyous Praise

DAY 28

SCRIPTURE REFERENCE: **PSALM 103:1-5 (CJB)**

Bless Adonai, my soul! Everything in me, bless His holy name! Bless Adonai, my soul, and forget none of His benefits! He forgives all your offenses, He heals all your diseases, He redeems your life from the pit, He surrounds you with grace and compassion, He contents you with good as long as you live, so that your youth is renewed like an eagle's.

Today is another opportunity for our soul to lift high praises to the Lord.

He delights as our soul pours out words of adoration!

Divine fellowship transpires when we praise.

Together, our fellowship brings sweetness!

Joyous Praise

DAY 29

Bless the Lord from the depths of our being.

Sing unto the Lord a new song from deep within.

Dance with all our might.

Our lips shout loudly of all Your benefits and mighty deeds.

Our God is alive! Our God is mighty to save! Our God is mighty to deliver!

SCRIPTURE REFERENCE: **PSALMS 98:1 (KJV)**

O sing unto the Lord a new song; for He hath done marvellous things: His right hand, and His holy arm, hath gotten Him the victory.

Joyous Praise

DAY 30

Scripture Reference: **Proverbs 10:22 (NAS)**

It is the blessing of the Lord that makes rich, and He adds no sorrow to it.

Let God's holy blessings fall upon you today.

When the blessings are from Him, they are pure.

Every blessing should bring a response of glowing praise from our lips!

Miracle Breakthroughs

Joyous Praise

DAY 31

SCRIPTURE REFERENCE: **PSALMS 30:5 (NAS)**

For His anger is but for a moment, His favor is for a lifetime; weeping may last for the night, but a shout of joy comes in the morning.

SCRIPTURE REFERENCE: **PSALMS 35:27-28 (NAS)**

Let them shout for joy and rejoice, who favor my vindication; and let them say continually, "The Lord be magnified, Who delights in the prosperity of His servant." And my tongue shall declare Your righteousness and Your praise all day long.

When the children of Israel crossed over into the land of promise, it was a time of deliverance from the former into the new. That crossing meant it was time to eat of the abundant produce of the promised land...no more manna!

(Continued on next page...)

Hold on to the promise until it manifests!

During your journey to the promise, REJOICE!

When your promise does manifest, REJOICE!

Rejoice the whole way through to the fulfillment of your heart's desires.

Your Abba delights in your praise! He is worthy of every word uttered in praise!

SCRIPTURE REFERENCE: **HEBREWS 13:5 (KJV)**

...for he hath said, "I will never leave thee, nor forsake thee."

Selah!

- Chapter Four -

My Beloved

Miracle Breakthroughs

My Beloved

DAY 1

M = Many
I = Incredible
R = Rapid
A = Accelerated
C = Cleansing
L = Leveling
E = Encounters

Today is a new day...a new beginning. As you start this day, begin it fresh and renewed...just as the Jews when they passed over the Red Sea and left Egypt behind.

Each day, hear your Beloved's voice calling you forth into the fullness of His love...

"Come all who long for more of Me. I will give you rest as you take each step towards Me...towards the promise of creating and walking step by step with Me, your Bridegroom indeed. You will experience more of Me so you can give more of Me to those in need."

(Continued on next page...)

Miracle Breakthroughs

SCRIPTURE REFERENCE: **ECCLESIASTES 3:11 (KJV)**

He hath made every thing beautiful in his time.

My Beloved

DAY 2

POEM:

> My soul longs for my Beloved.
> Early in the morning, His face I seek.
> His light shines through the darkness,
> Setting ablaze my soul.
>
> I called for my Beloved,
> And His love answered,
> Making me whole.

May His unfailing love be your first waking thought!

SCRIPTURE REFERENCE: **PSALMS 143:8 (CJB)**

Make me hear of your love in the morning, because I rely on you. Make me know the way I should walk, because I entrust myself to you.

My Beloved

DAY 3

The face of our Beloved...

Eyes... piercing deeply with kindness.
Ears... listening intently.
Nose... breathing so sweetly.
Mouth... kissing so tenderly.

Jesus/Yeshua, embrace us... face to face... heart to heart...

Melt us into one.

YOU are all we want!

SCRIPTURE REFERENCE: **SONG OF SOLOMON 5:2 (NAS)**

I was asleep but my heart was awake. A voice! My beloved was knocking: 'Open to me, my sister, my darling, My dove, my perfect one!...'

My Beloved

DAY 4

Your innocent dance delights the King.

Your movement catches His eye.

Your free expression melts His heart.

All comes alive in the presence of the King!

SCRIPTURE REFERENCE: **PSALMS 16:3 (NAS)**

As for the saints who are in the earth, they are the majestic ones in whom is all my delight.

Miracle Breakthroughs

My Beloved

DAY 5

POEM:

You and me, my Beloved, this season is so divine.
Separated for a purpose beyond my mind.
The future is one of a kind.
I am my Beloved's, and He is mine.

Friends, our bridegroom is inviting. Surrender!

SCRIPTURE REFERENCE: **LEVITICUS 20:26 (NAS)**

Thus you are to be holy to Me, for I the Lord am holy; and I have set you apart from the peoples to be Mine.

My Beloved

DAY 6

I declare the atmosphere of your day be enraptured with the drawing of your Bridegroom (Jesus/Yeshua) as you run into His chambers.

His love is better than life itself!

Let His love deeply saturate you, making you whole.

It is your time of healing and restoration.

Prepare for the wedding feast!

SCRIPTURE REFERENCE: **SONG OF SOLOMON 1:1-4 (NAS)**

The Song of Songs, which is Solomon's. May he kiss me with the kisses of his mouth! For your love is better than wine. Your oils have a pleasing fragrance, Your name is like purified oil; therefore the maidens love you. Draw me after you and let us run together! The king has brought me into his chambers. We will rejoice in you and be glad; we will extol your love more than wine. Rightly do they love you.

My Beloved

DAY 7

The Sabbath Rest: a special time appointed with your Beloved.

"Come away and let Me whisper sweetness in your ears, give you pleasantries to eat and refresh your soul with My goodness."

Your love, Jesus/Yeshua, is a canopy...surrounding us. Let us rest in this special Sabbath moment.

SCRIPTURE REFERENCE: **SONG OF SOLOMON 2:3-4 (KJV)**

As the apple tree among the trees of the wood, so is my beloved among the sons. I sat down under his shadow with great delight, and his fruit was sweet to my taste. He brought me to the banqueting house, and his banner over me was love.

My Beloved

DAY 8

SCRIPTURE REFERENCE: **SONG OF SOLOMON 5:16 (NAS)**

His mouth is full of sweetness. And he is wholly desirable. This is my beloved and this is my friend, O daughters of Jerusalem.

My whole being rests in the safety of Your wholeness, my first love, Jesus/Yeshua!

Let the sweet words He joyfully sings over you melt your heart.

Interestingly enough, His mouth, full of sweetness, is tied to Him being wholly desirable.

Are we desirable? With Christ being our example, we are to be as He is to others.

Let the fire of God purify your soul so that your mind and mouth speak sweetness.

My Beloved

DAY 9

Beloved Jesus/Yeshua, Your love has entirely washed over us. Your name is sweet on our lips.

Your desire is for us and we yearn for you, our Beloved.

SCRIPTURE REFERENCE: **SONG OF SOLOMON 7:10 (NAS)**

I am my beloved's, and his desire is for me.

My Beloved

DAY 10

In this new day, those seeking the heart of God will resolve to seek His presence, not merely His power.

It is time for a deeper intimacy to be evident in our desires, our actions, and our worship. It is time to commune as the Bridegroom and Bride. It is time for oneness like we've never known before.

So let God's face be our focus and let us guard the closeness we have with Him.

As our day progresses, let desire for greater passion arise so we stay nestled in Him. Our thoughts are set on Our Beloved. Our eyes are set on Our Beloved. Our ears are listening for Our Beloved. Our hearts long for the touch of Our Beloved.

SCRIPTURE REFERENCE: **SONG OF SOLOMON 5:8 (NAS)**

I adjure you, O daughters of Jerusalem, if you find my beloved, as to what you will tell him: for I am lovesick.

My Beloved

DAY 11

To know you, Jesus/Yeshua, is to love You.

Your voice soothes our soul.

Your eyes melt our hearts.

Your touch makes us feel secure and safe.

We will stay in Your presence the whole day through, our hands joined.

SCRIPTURE REFERENCE: **SONG OF SOLOMON 8:6-7 (NAS)**

Put me like a seal over your heart, like a seal on your arm. For love is as strong as death, jealousy is as severe as Sheol; its flashes are flashes of fire, the very flame of the Lord. Many waters cannot quench love...

My Beloved

DAY 12

In the stillness of your love, our Beloved, we will stay and listen to your heartbeat. Our spirit and soul will memorize its rhythm. Then, we will know a counterfeit.

We want to walk and live what is true. We want to stay on the path labeled YOU.

Our Beloved, you are the best! Our eyes don't look to another.

SCRIPTURE REFERENCE: **PSALMS 119:9-12 (NAS)**

How can a young man keep his way pure? By keeping it according to Your word. With all my heart I have sought You; do not let me wander from Your commandments. Your word I have treasured in my heart, that I may not sin against You. Blessed are You, O LORD; teach me Your statutes.

My Beloved

DAY 13

Our soul arises early in the morning to seek Your face, our Beloved.

We long to see the light in Your eye as You wink at us.

Just one glance at You, Beloved, and all seems right in our world. Our soul has found its resting place.

Now, our day can go forth in Your praise.

You will be on our mind and our lips will speak of Your delight.

Our Beloved loves us. This promise we can hold true.

SCRIPTURE REFERENCE: **PSALMS 116:7 (NAS)**

Return to your rest, O my soul, for the Lord has dealt bountifully with you.

My Beloved

DAY 14

One day, I had a deep, analytical, energizing talk with a girlfriend. We were discussing how "fullness" is frequently used to refer to ministry and coming into your full capabilities. She said "fullness" to her meant Christ-like. I really like that definition!

Religion focuses on the outward. God chases after the heart. May we run so deep into God's heart that people see without question that we are one of His. When the heart of the Father is seen in our actions instead of our own will, it is then that pure and righteous ministry naturally flows. That would be the true fullness of intimacy with our Beloved!

SCRIPTURE REFERENCE: *JOHN 14:11-12 (KJV)*

Believe me that I am in the Father, and the Father in me: or else believe me for the very works' sake. Verily, verily, I say unto you, He that believeth on me, the works that I do shall he do also; and greater works than these shall he do; because I go unto my Father.

My Beloved

DAY 15

SCRIPTURE REFERENCE: **NUMBERS 6:24-26 (NAS)**

The Lord bless you, and keep you; the Lord make His face shine on you, and be gracious to you; the Lord lift up His countenance on you, and give you peace.

Gaze upon the One we pierced, whose blood cried out forgiveness. Behold the beauty of His face that shines night and day upon you. Your precious Beloved truly desires for your soul to prosper and be at peace!

His look of love is one that is never forgotten.

SCRIPTURE REFERENCE: **REVELATION 5:9 (NAS)**

And they sang a new song saying, Worthy are You to take the book and to break its seals; for You were slain, and purchased for God with Your blood men from every tribe and tongue and people and nation.

My Beloved

DAY 16

God's tender mercies never fail or fade. They are fresh for you every morning when you awaken.

Cry out for mercy and your Bridegroom's tender heart will answer, satisfying your longing.

May you experience His kind mercy today, fulfilling your every need.

SCRIPTURE REFERENCE: **LAMENTATIONS 3:20-23 (NAS)**

Surely my soul remembers and is bowed down within me. This I recall to my mind, therefore I have hope. The Lord's loving kindnesses indeed never cease, for His compassions never fail. They are new every morning; great is Your faithfulness.

My Beloved

DAY 17

The greatest reason for living is just being in fellowship with Abba.

The greatest union in life is through fellowship.

We can be in relationship with someone but not have fellowship.

I pray these thoughts will spark a desire to go deeper, to see deeper, and to know deeper the great yearning of Abba's heart for you and the world.

May the unity of fellowship shine upon you. May you reflect your Beloved!

SCRIPTURE REFERENCE: **PHILEMON 1:6 (CJB)**

I pray that the fellowship based on your commitment will produce full understanding of every good thing that is ours in union with the Messiah.

My Beloved

DAY 18

Divine love heals every hurt.

Divine love is fuel for the soul.

Divine love allows freedom of expression.

All comes alive in the love received from our Beloved!

May every fiber of your being be vitalized with your Beloved's endearing love.

SCRIPTURE REFERENCE: **PSALMS 119:149 (MSG)**

In your love, listen to me; in your justice, God, keep me alive.

My Beloved

DAY 19

Religion is about works.

Resting is about stilling your spirit and soul.

Are you driven by doing works?

Relax in the arms of your Beloved and restfully stay in rhythm with Him. Move with Him, and be one with Him.

SCRIPTURE REFERENCE: **ACTS 17:28 (KJV)**

For in him we live, and move, and have our being...

My Beloved

DAY 20

Rest in the satisfaction from knowing that your Beloved will provide your every need, according to His will.

His peace is enough.

His grace is enough.

His provision is enough.

His arms of comfort are enough.

His love is enough.

Be settled in the "enough" of a Beloved whose eyes are fixed on you!

SCRIPTURE REFERENCE: **I TIMOTHY 6:6 (NAS)**

But godliness actually is a means of great gain when accompanied by contentment.

My Beloved

DAY 21

Father is the fountain of life that never runs dry. When we thirst for Him and behold Him, all things are made new.

Let our ears be tuned to His voice, and hear His words above all else.

His words bring us beauty and make us whole!

He truly is the Alpha and Omega, the beginning and the end. His promises can be trusted through all of life's journeys:

> ...the winding roads,
> ...the rushing waters,
> ...the desert dry,
> ...the mountain tops,
> ...the valleys low.

Let your Beloved's living waters quench and satisfy your dry and thirsty soul!

(Continued on next page...)

SCRIPTURE REFERENCE: **REVELATION 21:5-6 (KJV)**

And He that sat upon the throne said, Behold, I make all things new. And He said unto me, write: for these words are true and faithful. And He said unto me, it is done. I am Alpha and Omega, the beginning and the end. I will give unto him that is athirst of the fountain of the water of life freely.

My Beloved

DAY 22

May you meet your Lover with fresh eyes every morning, and hear His voice anew.

May your soul drink deeply of His words.

"Come away, my beloved, let my Sabbath rest drench you."

The Sabbath rest is the state in which you are called to live.

He wants to captivate you wholly!!

SCRIPTURE REFERENCE: **HEBREWS 4:9-11 (NAS)**

So there remains a Sabbath rest for the people of God. For the one who has entered His rest has himself also rested from his works, as God did from His. Therefore let us be diligent to enter that rest, so that no one will fall...

My Beloved

DAY 23

SCRIPTURE REFERENCE: **SONG OF SOLOMON 2:3-4 (NAS)**

Like an apple tree among the trees of the forest, so is my beloved among the young men. In His shade I took great delight and sat down, and His fruit was sweet to my taste. He has brought me to His banquet hall, and His banner over me is love.

Your Beloved is wooing you to dine.

He has placed the best in front of you.

All that remains is for you to pull up the chair and sit at His table.

He is ready to take you to the next level of making all things new!

Let His love saturate you with renewed strength and peace of mind and greater joy in your salvation.

My Beloved

DAY 24

SCRIPTURE REFERENCE: **PSALMS 32:8 (NAS)**

I will instruct you and teach you in the way which you should go; I will counsel you with My eye upon you.

It is a delight to wake up in the morning greeting Abba as He gives instructions for what to do today.

His eye watches over your sleep and his word is nigh, written on the tablet of your heart.

Arise and shine as you walk out His counsel.

SCRIPTURE REFERENCE: **ISAIAH 60:1 (KJV)**

Arise, shine; for thy light is come, and the glory of the Lord is risen upon thee.

My Beloved

DAY 25

It is time for that which has been broken to be fixed!

It is time for a house cleaning to make room for goodness to be poured out!

Our Bridegroom is intently smiling in anticipation.

It is time to reap! We are about to receive showers of blessings!

SCRIPTURE REFERENCE: **GALATIANS. 6:9 (NAS)**

Let us not lose heart in doing good, for in due time we will reap if we do not grow weary.

My Beloved

DAY 26

SCRIPTURE REFERENCE: SONG OF SOLOMON 2:14-16 (NAS)

O my dove, in the clefts of the rock, in the secret place of the steep pathway, let me see your form, let me hear your voice; for your voice is sweet, and your form is lovely. Catch the foxes for us, the little foxes that are ruining the vineyards, while our vineyards are in blossom. My beloved is mine, and I am his; he pastures his flock among the lilies.

Ask Holy Spirit to show you any "foxes" that are hindering or pulling you away from your Beloved's voice and ways.

Truly, we want to be in His safety and blossom!

My Beloved

DAY 27

Jesus/Yeshua is gently persistent, always seeking you out...ever inviting.

Ask for Holy Spirit's help to stay in a place of communion throughout the day, dialoging back and forth.

That fellowship is like a five-star meal every day... delectable and rewarding!

SCRIPTURE REFERENCE: **REVELATION 3:20 (CJB)**

Here, I'm standing at the door, knocking. If someone hears my voice and opens the door, I will come in to him and eat with him, and he will eat with me.

(Continued on next page...)

Miracle Breakthroughs

SCRIPTURE REFERENCE: **MATTHEW 7:7-8 (CJB)**

Keep asking, and it will be given to you; keep seeking, and you will find; keep knocking, and the door will be opened to you. For everyone who keeps asking receives; he who keeps seeking finds; and to him who keeps knocking, the door will be opened.

My Beloved

DAY 28

SCRIPTURE REFERENCE: **MATTHEW 6:21 (NAS)**

for where your treasure is, there your heart will be also.

The greatest joy in our life is loving Jesus/Yeshua, our treasure. There are many ways to express that love daily.

This treasure is the fairest of ten thousands, a Bridegroom who always has your back, surrounds you with truth, and speaks words of life to you every moment of the day. We fall in love with Him, over and over again.

Each day, find a special way to treasure your Treasure.

My Beloved

DAY 29

You are beautiful beyond description to your Beloved.

When your Beloved looks at you, He sees how His love has made you blossom!

You have been loved to life abundantly!

SCRIPTURE REFERENCE: **JEREMIAH 31:3 (KJV)**

The Lord hath appeared of old unto me, saying, Yea, I have loved thee with an everlasting love: therefore with lovingkindness have I drawn thee.

My Beloved

DAY 30

POEM:

<u>Jesus/Yeshua, My Beloved</u>

Melt my heart,
Make it tender.
Fill every part,
With your wonder.

Your gazing eyes,
Your sweet caress,
Leaves me feeling,
Quite precious.

Your boundless love,
Makes me teary-eyed,
I want to be,
your eternal bride!

(Continued on next page...)

Miracle Breakthroughs

Today, feel Heaven's beat and dance with new rhythm. All is aligning to a new order with our Bridegroom and each other. The Bride is making herself ready and her Father is helping!

SCRIPTURE REFERENCE: **REVELATION 19:7 (NAS)**

Let us rejoice and be glad and give the glory to Him, for the marriage of the Lamb has come and His bride has made herself ready.

My Beloved

DAY 31

Chase the Blesser, and the blessing will follow.

Chase the Bridegroom, and the inheritance will follow.

We are desperate for you, our Love.

We seek YOU alone, above all else.

Our hearts are yours, and it is to your delight to give richly to us.

Let us smile together, laugh together, and just "be" together. Let us stay together forever, hearts beating as one.

SCRIPTURE REFERENCE: **DEUTERONOMY 28:2 (NAS)**

All these blessings will come upon you and overtake you if you obey the Lord your God.

Selah!

Miracle Breakthroughs

ABOUT THE AUTHOR

Sara Zimmer has been raised in and around the ministry all of her life. Growing up in a pastor's home, her parents, Chuck and Ruth Zimmer, taught her to develop and cultivate an intimate relationship with Abba Father. This has led to living a life of unconditional love towards others.

Sara Zimmer

As a young lady, Sara attended and graduated Bible school and became an ordained minister. Her professional career has led her into service in many different capacities and organizations. Some of these range from radio broadcasting, where she was a director and an on-air personality, to various non-profit organizations, where she was in administration, to participating in outreach missions trips to Israel, Africa, Guatemala, and other locations. But she knows that, above all else, Abba desires for us to maintain an intimate fellowship with Him as a number one priority…before Christian service.

Throughout her corporate career, she has listened to the voice of Holy Spirit and allowed Him to guide her in daily activities and interactions. As a trainer for a Fortune 500 company, this surrender has been recognized by peers and administrators alike for its wisdom and favor.

Miracle Breakthroughs

Sara has unique giftings that enable her to pull out and nurture a person's authentic self, bypassing any masks or facades that they are hiding behind and meeting them at their point of need. Her prophetic anointing offers her a practical, down-to-earth approach to overcoming many of the hurdles that Christians face today.

A Tulsa, Oklahoma resident, Sara is a strong supporter of Israel and Jerusalem, and has come into an understanding of the Hebraic roots of Christianity. She has a deep passion for prophetic dancing, and enjoys writing and singing prophetic songs and poems.

> *"My true heart's desire is to see people free from the emotional hurts, pains, and bondages of the past so they can be who they are called to be and walk in the freedom that salvation brings."*
> -Sara Zimmer

For speaking engagements or additional information, please email: info@explosivebreakthrough.org
or visit:
www.ExplosiveBreakthrough.org

APPENDIX A:
Scripture References

Chapter One - Love 1

DAY 1 3
  Reference: **Mark 1:41-42 (NAS)**
DAY 2 5
  Reference: **Psalms 46:10 (KJV)**
  Reference: **1 John 4:8 (KJV)**
DAY 3 7
  Reference: **Jeremiah 31:3-4 (NAS)**
DAY 4 8
  Reference: **Luke 12:7 (CJB)**
DAY 5 9
  Reference: **Psalms 23:4 (NAS)**
DAY 6 10
  Reference: **John 3:16 (NAS)**
DAY 7 11
  Reference: **Psalms 119:114 (KJV)**
DAY 8 12
  Reference: **Matthew 25:40 (NAS)**
DAY 9 13
  Reference: **Proverbs 17:17 (NAS)**
DAY 10 14
  Reference: **Lamentations 3:22-23 (NAS)**
DAY 11 15
  Reference: **Matthew 7:12 (MSG)**
DAY 12 16
  Reference: **Psalms 12:6 (NAS)**
DAY 13 17
  Reference: **Psalms 121:1 (KJV)**
  Reference: **Hebrews 4:16 (NAS)**
DAY 14 19
  Reference: **2 Chronicles 16:9 (NAS)**

Appendix A: Scripture References

DAY 15 20
Reference: **Song of Solomon 1:16 (NAS)**

DAY 16 21
Reference: **Luke 10:27 (NAS)**

DAY 17 22
Reference: **Revelation 21:6 (NAS)**
Reference: **Matthew 26:38-39 (KJV)**

DAY 18 24
Reference: **Proverbs 10:22 (NAS)**
Reference: **James 1:17 (NAS)**

DAY 19 25
Reference: **Philippians 1:6 (NAS)**

DAY 20 26
Reference: **Hebrews 7:24-25 (NAS)**

DAY 21 27
Reference: **Psalms 92:1-2 (KJV)**

DAY 22 28
Reference: **Ezekiel 11:19-20 (KJV)**

DAY 23 29
Reference: **Philippians 4:8 (NAS)**

DAY 24 30
Reference: **John 15:9 (KJV)**

DAY 25 31
Reference: **Psalms 11:7 (NAS)**

DAY 26 32
Reference: **John 15:13 (NAS)**

DAY 27 33
Reference: **Isaiah 58:8 (NAS)**

DAY 28 34
Reference: **Matthew 5:16 (NAS)**

DAY 29 35
Reference: **Proverbs 22:1 (NAS)**

DAY 30 36
Reference: **Matthew 20:34 (NAS)**

DAY 31 37
Reference: **I John 4:18-19 (NAS)**

Appendix A: Scripture References

Chapter Two - Peace 39

DAY 1 41
   Reference: **Psalms 122:8 (CJB)**
   Reference: **Romans 8:28 (KJV)**

DAY 2 43
   Reference: **Isaiah 9:6-7 (KJV)**

DAY 3 44
   Reference: **Isaiah 32:16-17 (NAS)**

DAY 4 45
   Reference: **I Chronicles 16:31 (NAS)**
   Reference: **Psalms 118:24 (NAS)**
   Reference: **Exodus 14:14 (KJV)**

DAY 5 46
   Reference: **Romans 14:16-19 (NAS)**

DAY 6 47
   Reference: **Romans 8:6 (NAS)**

DAY 7 48
   Reference: **Numbers 6:24-26 (KJV)**

DAY 8 49
   Reference: **Isaiah 26:3 (NAS)**

DAY 9 50
   Reference: **Psalms 62:5 (KJV)**

DAY 10 51
   Reference: **Isaiah 14:7 (NAS)**

DAY 11 52
   Reference: **Psalms 16:5-6 (NAS)**

DAY 12 53
   Reference: **Isaiah 26:3 (KJV)**

DAY 13 54
   Reference: **Ephesians 4:1-3 (NAS)**

DAY 14 55
   Reference: **Job 22:21-22 (NAS)**
   Reference: **Romans 8:28 (KJV)**

Appendix A: Scripture References

DAY 15 56
   Reference: **2 Thessalonians 3:16 (CJB)**

DAY 16 57
   Reference: **Matthew 11:28-30 (NAS)**

DAY 17 58
   Reference: **Luke 11:36 (NAS)**

DAY 18 59
   Reference: **Matthew 18:12-14 (NAS)**
   Reference: **Luke 15:28-32 (MSG)**

DAY 19 61
   Reference: **Colossians 3:15 (NAS)**

DAY 20 62
   Reference: **Zechariah 8:16 (NAS)**

DAY 21 63
   Reference: **Exodus 14:13-14 (KJV)**

DAY 22 64
   Reference: **Matthew 5:8-9 (KJV)**

DAY 23 65
   Reference: **Proverbs 3:5-8 (CJB)**

DAY 24 66
   Reference: **Psalms 32:8 (NAS)**
   Reference: **Psalms 23:3 (MSG)**

DAY 25 67
   Reference: **Psalms 23:1-2 (NLT)**

DAY 26 68
   Reference: **Numbers 26:6 (NAS)**

DAY 27 69
   Reference: **John 14:26-27 (NAS)**

DAY 28 70
   Reference: **Joshua 1:9 (KJV)**

DAY 29 71
   Reference: **Numbers 13:30 (NAS)**

DAY 30 72
   Reference: **Psalms 27:4 (NAS)**

DAY 31 73
   Reference: **Song of Solomon 6:13 (MSG)**
   Reference: **Revelation 21:2 (KJV)**

Appendix A: Scripture References

Chapter Three - Joyous Praise 75

DAY 1 77
Reference: **Psalms 149:4-6 (KJV)**
DAY 2 78
Reference: **Psalms 35:27 (CJB)**
DAY 3 79
Reference: **Zephaniah 3:17 (CJB)**
DAY 4 80
Reference: **Psalms 126:1-2 (KJV)**
DAY 5 81
Reference: **Exodus 15:2 (NAS)**
DAY 6 82
Reference: **Revelation 14:7 (NAS)**
DAY 7 83
Reference: **Psalms 19:1 (NAS)**
DAY 8 84
Reference: **Isaiah 55:9-12 (NAS)**
DAY 9 86
Reference: **Luke 15:7 (NAS)**
DAY 10 87
Reference: **3 John 1:3-4 (NAS)**
DAY 11 88
Reference: **I Chronicles 16:29-30 (KJV)**
DAY 12 89
Reference: **Isaiah 35:10 (NAS)**
DAY 13 90
Reference: **Psalms 57:8-11 (NAS)**
DAY 14 91
Reference: **Jeremiah 31:13 (NAS)**
DAY 15 92
Reference: **2 Samuel 6:14-15 (KJV)**

Appendix A: Scripture References

DAY 16 93
   Reference: **Psalms 32:11 (NAS)**
   Reference: **Philippians 4:4 (KJV)**

DAY 17 94
   Reference: **Psalms 33:3 (CJB)**

DAY 18 95
   Reference: **Psalms 119:171 (NAS)**

DAY 19 96
   Reference: **Psalms 5:3 (NAS)**

DAY 20 97
   Reference: **Isaiah 56:7 (NAS)**

DAY 21 98
   Reference: **Psalms 22:3-4 (NAS)**

DAY 22 99
   Reference: **I Chronicles 16:8-10 (CJB)**

DAY 23 100
   Reference: **Proverbs 17:22 (KJV)**

DAY 24 101
   Reference: **Psalm 141:2 (CJB)**

DAY 25 102
   Reference: **Psalm 23 (KJV)**

DAY 26 103
   Reference: **Psalms 30:11-12 (CJB)**

DAY 27 104
   Reference: **Psalms 100:4 (KJV)**

DAY 28 105
   Reference: **Psalm 103:1-5 (CJB)**

DAY 29 106
   Reference: **Psalms 98:1 (KJV)**

DAY 30 107
   Reference: **Proverbs 10:22 (NAS)**

DAY 31 108
   Reference: **Psalms 30:5 (NAS)**
   Reference: **Psalms 35:27-28 (NAS)**
   Reference: **Hebrews 13:5 (KJV)**

Appendix A: Scripture References

Chapter Four - My Beloved 111

DAY 1 113
Reference: **Ecclesiastes 3:11 (KJV)**
DAY 2 115
Reference: **Psalms 143:8 (CJB)**
DAY 3 116
Reference: **Song of Solomon 5:2 (NAS)**
DAY 4 117
Reference: **Psalms 16:3 (NAS)**
DAY 5 118
Reference: **Leviticus 20:26 (NAS)**
DAY 6 119
Reference: **Song of Solomon 1:1-4 (NAS)**
DAY 7 120
Reference: **Song of Solomon 2:3-4 (KJV)**
DAY 8 121
Reference: **Song of Solomon 5:16 (NAS)**
DAY 9 122
Reference: **Song of Solomon 7:10 (NAS)**
DAY 10 123
Reference: **Song of Solomon 5:8 (NAS)**
DAY 11 124
Reference: **Song of Solomon 8:6-7 (NAS)**
DAY 12 125
Reference: **Psalms 119:9-12 (NAS)**
DAY 13 126
Reference: **Psalms 116:7 (NAS)**
DAY 14 127
Reference: **John 14:11-12 (KJV)**
DAY 15 128
Reference: **Numbers 6:24-26 (NAS)**
Reference: **Revelation 5:9 (NAS)**

Appendix A: Scripture References

DAY 16 129
Reference: **Lamentations 3:20-23 (NAS)**

DAY 17 130
Reference: **Philemon 1:6 (CJB)**

DAY 18 131
Reference: **Psalms 119:149 (MSG)**

DAY 19 132
Reference: **Acts 17:28 (KJV)**

DAY 20 133
Reference: **I Timothy 6:6 (NAS)**

DAY 21 134
Reference: **Revelation 21:5-6 (KJV)**

DAY 22 136
Reference: **Hebrews 4:9-11 (NAS)**

DAY 23 137
Reference: **Song of Solomon 2:3-4 (NAS)**

DAY 24 138
Reference: **Psalms 32:8 (NAS)**
Reference: **Isaiah 60:1 (KJV)**

DAY 25 139
Reference: **Galatians. 6:9 (NAS)**

DAY 26 140
Reference: **Song of Solomon 2:14-16 (NAS)**

DAY 27 141
Reference: **Revelation 3:20 (CJB)**
Reference: **Matthew 7:7-8 (CJB)**

DAY 28 143
Reference: **Matthew 6:21 (NAS)**

DAY 29 144
Reference: **Jeremiah 31:3 (KJV)**

DAY 30 145
Reference: **Revelation 19:7 (NAS)**

DAY 31 147
Reference: **Deuteronomy 28:2 (NAS)**

Order Form
MIRACLE BREAKTHROUGHS
~ Volume I

Name: _____

Address: _____

City/State/Zip: _____

Phone: _____

Email: _____

Miracle Breakthroughs Vol. 1 ($15.00 each) $ _____

\+ Tax (Oklahoma addresses add 8.5%) $ _____

\+ Shipping ($4.95 + $2.00 for each additional copy) $ _____

= Total: $ _____

Method of Payment

☐ **Check** (Check No: _____)

☐ **Credit Card** (Card Type: _____)

Card Number: _____

Exp. Date: _____ Security Code: _____

Signature/Date: _____

Please mail this form to:
Explosive Breakthrough Publishing, LLC
P.O. Box 2522, Broken Arrow, OK 74013

(Please allow 2-3 weeks for processing. Bulk pricing available.
Email for details: info@explosivebreakthrough.org)

Order online at
www.ExplosiveBreakthrough.org